The Wonderful World of

LADYBUGS

Mimi Jones

Dedicated to all who love ladybugs!

ISBN 978-1-958985-09-0

www.joeysavestheday.com

A Mimi Book

Welcome to the Wonderful World of Ladybugs!

Ladybugs have two sets of wings.

The forewings are called the elytra wings.
The elytra wings are the hard colorful shell
that protects the light wings underneath.

www.ingramcontent.com/pod-product-compliance
Lightning Source LLC
Chambersburg PA
CBHW060839270326
41933CB00002B/139

Name: _____

Color the ladybug.

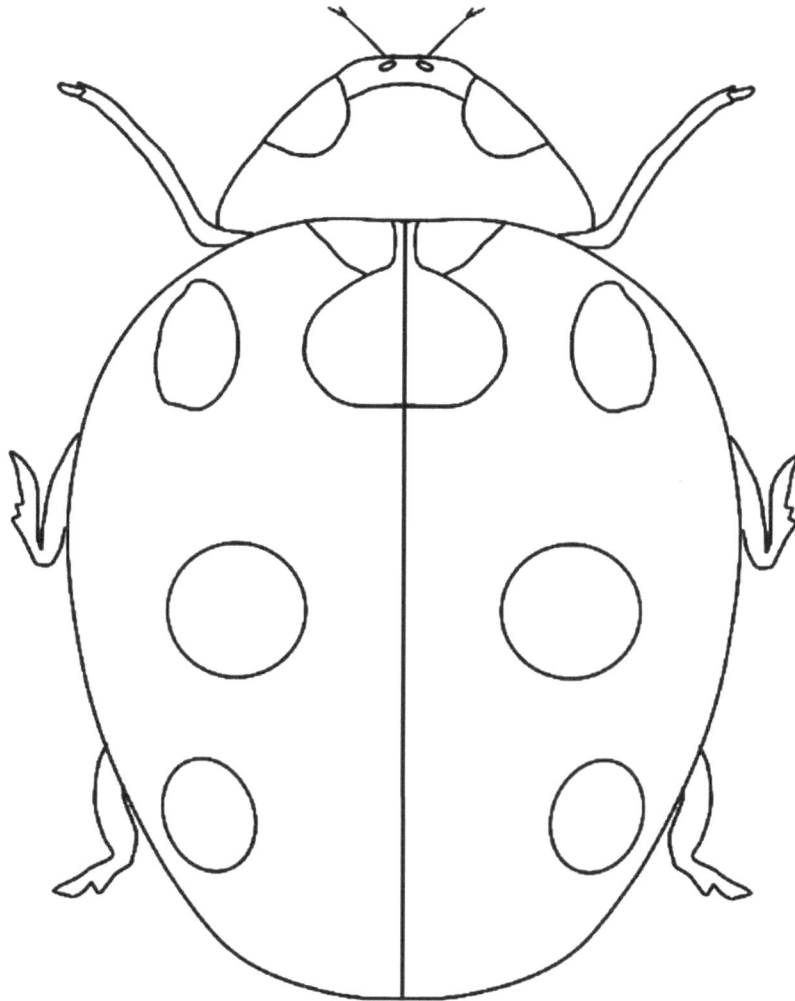

**How many ladybugs
do you see?**

The end!

What is a group of ladybugs called?

As she was thinking, she saw the light at the other end of that dreadful old shoe. So, she started crawling back towards the light. Once she reached the back end of that shoe, she crawled up and made her way to the top of the shoe. She finally figured out just what to do. She opened her wings and started to fly up high towards the sky!

Short story:

There once was a ladybug who didn't know what to do, for she got caught inside of an old dreadful shoe. She tried to climb up the inside of the shoe. But she couldn't figure out just what to do. She thought maybe if she went to the dark end of the shoe, she'd find her way out, but no such luck. She sat there in the dark thinking, how will I get out?

Ladybugs hibernate in the winter.

Ladybugs have six legs.

Ladybugs use their feet
and antennae to smell with.

sniff sniff

The body of a ladybug has three parts:

- **The head**
- **The thorax**
- **The abdomen**

Ladybugs are invertebrates.

Invertebrate means they
don't have a backbone.

Ladybugs are cold-blooded and need a lot of heat to survive.

A baby ladybug is
called a larva.

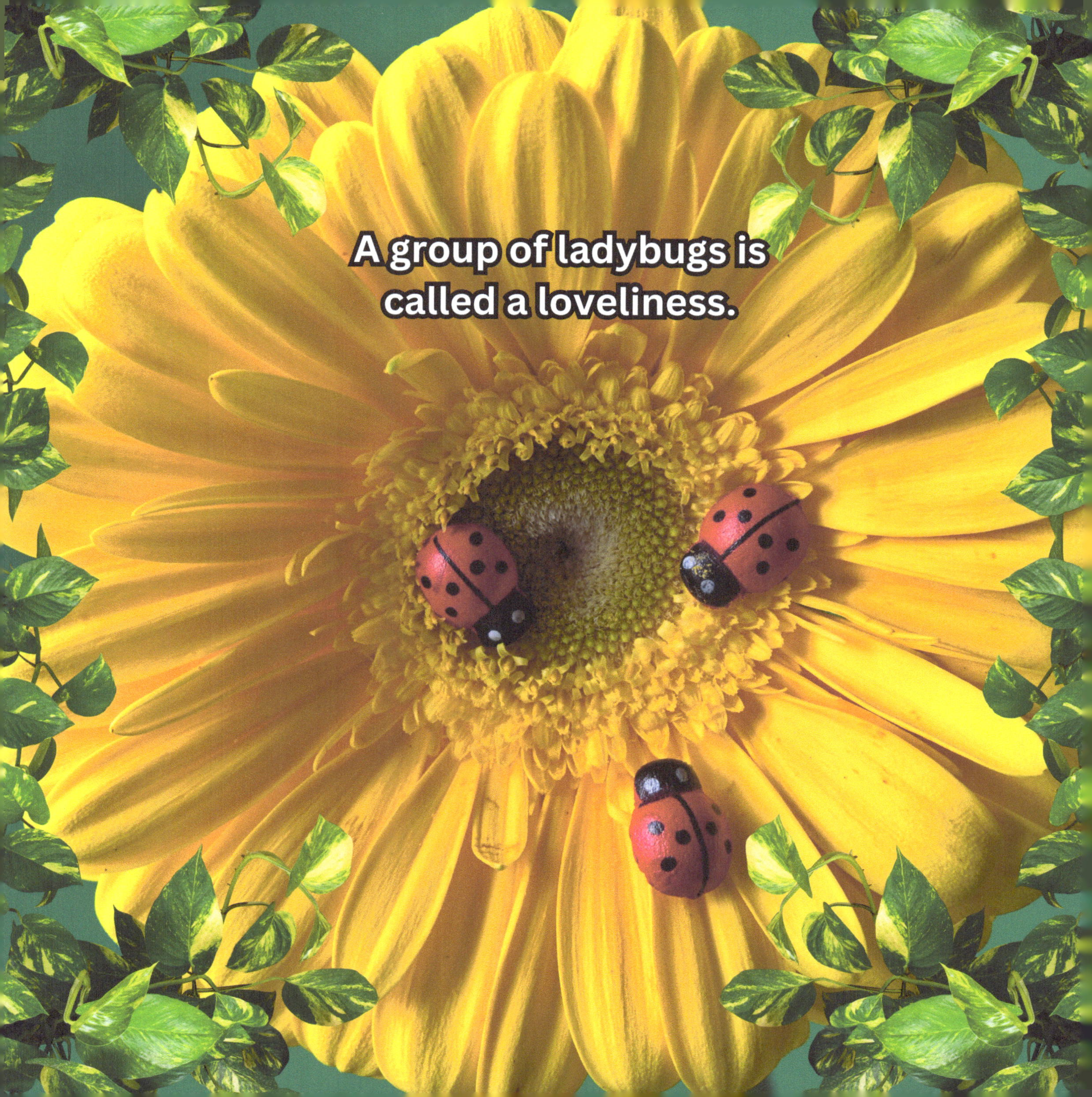

A group of ladybugs is called a loveliness.

Ladybugs are mostly diurnal.

Diurnal means
being active during
the daytime

Ladybugs can be found living
on all of the continents
except Antarctica.

There are over 5000
different types of ladybugs.

Here is a list of some different types of ladybugs:

- Convergent lady beetle
- Eyed ladybug
- Large leaf eating ladybug
- Twenty-spotted lady beetle
- Two-spot ladybird

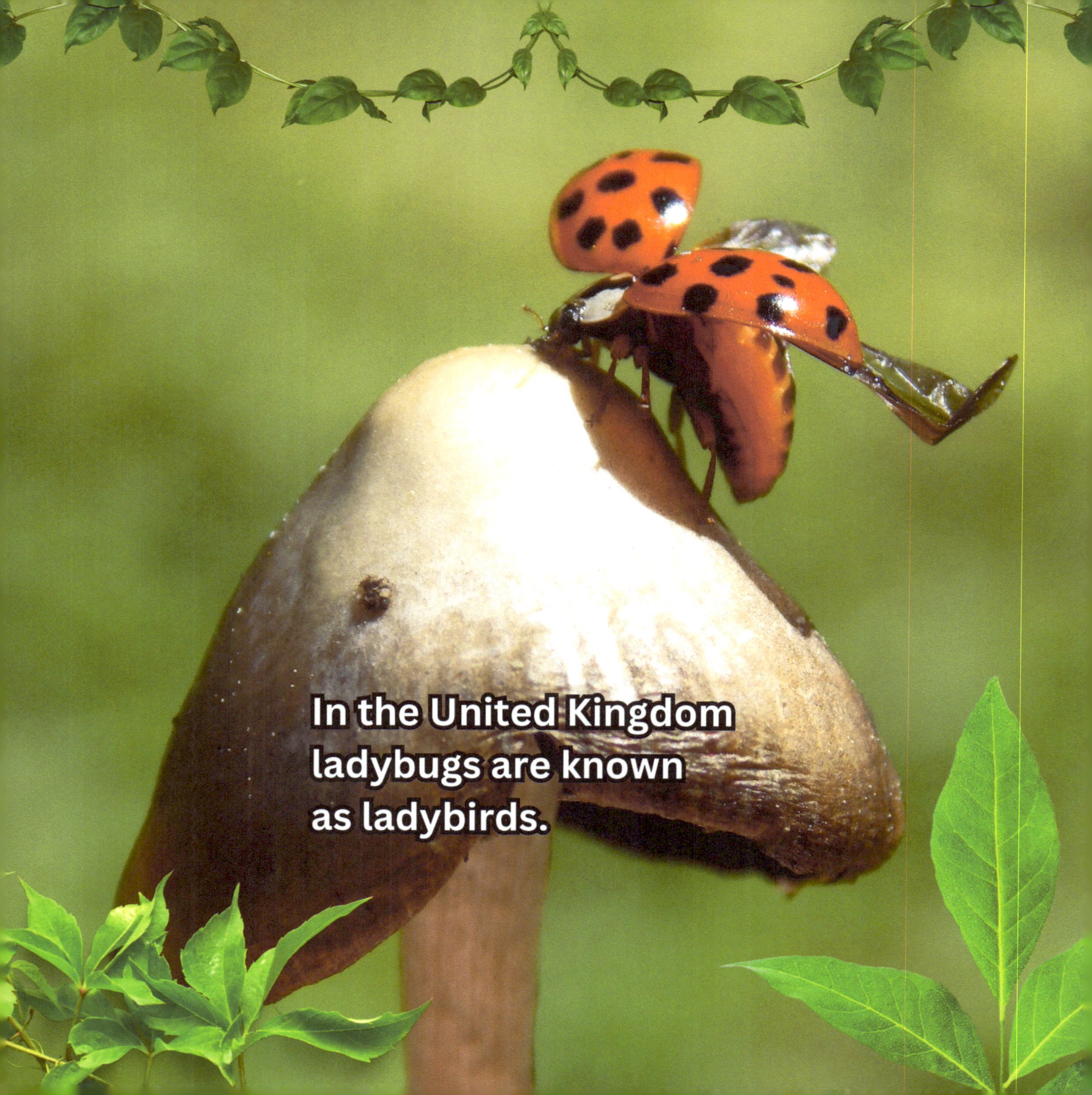

In the United Kingdom
ladybugs are known
as ladybirds.

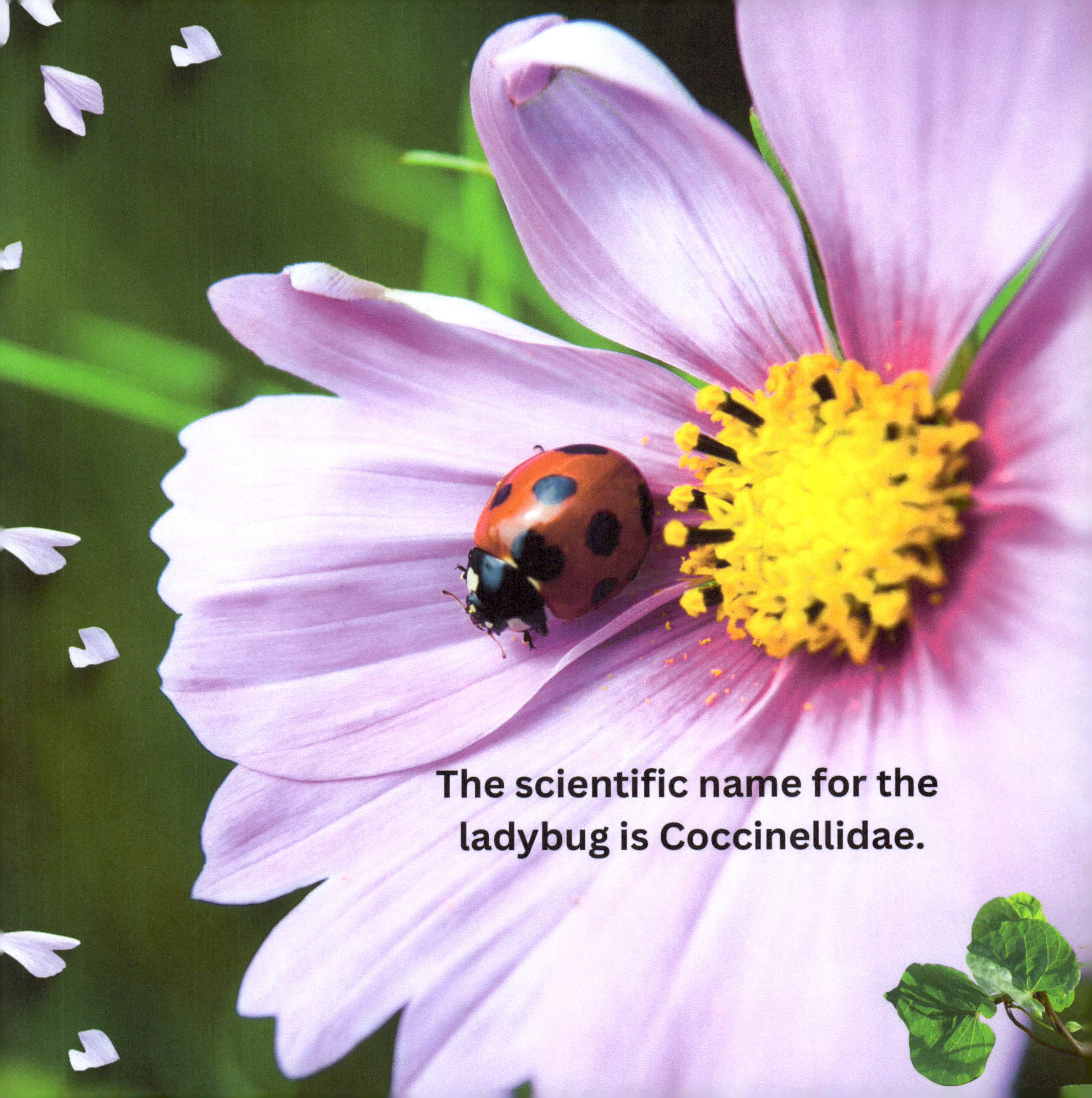

The scientific name for the
ladybug is Coccinellidae.

Ladybugs are from
the beetle family.

Life Cycle of a ladybug

Eggs

Larva

Pupa

Adult

Ladybugs have two eyes.

Ladybugs carry pollen
from plant to plant.

Ladybugs are pollinators.

Most ladybugs are omnivorse.
They eat small insects and plants.

Most ladybugs are red, orange, or yellow with black spots.